To all who enjoy this story.
There is a "Buttons" in every pet and a "Tammy" in every child.

Michael Terence Publishing

"I want a cat, mummy," said Tammy.

"They need to be looked after well Tammy," said mummy, "even if you don't feel like it."

"I know," said Tammy. "I will," she promised.

"OK," said mummy, "let's see what daddy thinks."

"Oh, thank you, mummy," said Tammy.

The next day, mummy, daddy and Tammy visited the pet shop.

There were so many animals to choose from.

There were dogs, birds, fish, rabbits, hamsters, guinea pigs, mice and even snakes...

hamster

fish

Dog

Bird

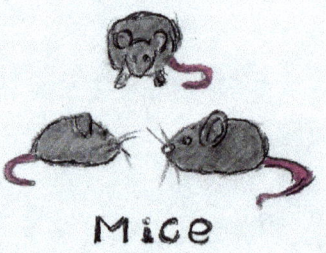
Mice

snake   rabbit

...but Tammy wanted a cat.

She chose a little Tabby cat. He was a tiny kitten. Only eight weeks old. He had six tiny toes on his front left paw.

He was a special little kitten, sitting all alone in the corner of the big cage. No other kittens were playing with him. Tammy felt sorry for him.

"I will take care of you," she thought.

Mummy and daddy helped Tammy choose all the things she would need for her new kitten: a bed, a blanket, a feeding bowl, food, a litter tray, cat litter, a scoop, a scratching post, a toy and a pet carrier.

They were then ready to take their new pet home.

BED BASKET

SCOOP

LETTER TRAY

CAT CARRIER

TOY MOUSE

SCRATCHING POST

BALL OF STRING

Tammy was very excited.

The little kitten was a bit nervous when he arrived at his new home, but he soon settled in.

Tammy named him Buttons.

He was so soft and loved to snuggle on Tammy's lap.

Every day he grew bigger and stronger.

He was very playful and loved to explore all over the house.

Sometimes Tammy wouldn't know where he was. He could be under a bed, behind a sofa or, even in the laundry basket.

He was so much fun and very good at Hide and Seek!

When he was older, Tammy took Buttons out in the garden for the very first time.

Buttons found this a bit scary. All the sounds were new. The feel of the air and wind was new, but he felt safe because Tammy was with him.

She showed him the garden and he slowly relaxed and began to enjoy it. He jumped and rolled in the grass. He ate some grass too. When Tammy saw him walking through the grass, she thought he looked like a little tiger!

He sniffed around... lots of new smells. This was a big adventure for him. He and Tammy really enjoyed it.

Each time Buttons went in the garden, he became braver.

Sometimes he would go out even if Tammy was not with him.

He wasn't scared anymore but,
of course,
he always loved it best
when Tammy was with him.

Six years passed. Buttons grew into a handsome cat, always very playful and adventurous. Tammy grew from a cute little girl into a pretty teenager.

She was very busy at school but always loved spending time with her Buttons.

During weekends and holidays was when Tammy spent a long time playing with Buttons in the garden.

He would leap about excitedly then lay down in the sun to rest. These were the best times.

It was on just one such day, during a school holiday that Tammy and Buttons were playing in the garden.

When Tammy had to go inside for lunch, she let Buttons stay in the garden, lazing on the cool grass in the warmth of the sunshine.

But, that day, something most strange happened.

When Tammy went back outside, Buttons was not there. He had not gone back inside either. He had gone...

Tammy, mummy and daddy searched everywhere. They called and called him, "Buttons! Buttons! Pssss pssss pssss pssss," but he did not come back.

Where was he? What happened?

It was terrible. Buttons had disappeared.
Tammy was so sad and worried.

Buttons was so scared. He was lost.

Why did I go exploring?" thought Buttons. He had jumped over the garden wall when Tammy was inside having her lunch.

He felt brave and excited at first and he went further and further, but when he started to meet some unkind people and some unfriendly animals, he began to wish he had stayed in his garden.

Some animals were wild and were not nice to him at all. Some had orange fur with a pointy nose and would always try to fight him.

Buttons had to run fast and hide a lot, but it wasn't fun like it was with Tammy.

This was scary.

He didn't like it at all.

Buttons knew he was lost. He no longer felt brave or excited. He felt afraid and very alone. He was also cold and hungry. "Where is my Tammy?" he thought as he hid under a bush.

Tammy was home, gazing sadly out of a window, painfully thinking, "Where are you Buttons?

Where did you go?"

Tammy and mummy put up posters of their lost cat, Buttons, but no one responded to them. The days passed into weeks. Buttons did not come home.

Tammy always thought of him and wondered where he was.

"Are you OK, Buttons?" "Are you dead or alive?" "Why don't you come home?"

So many questions and such sadness filled Tammy's heart every day.

Buttons still could not find Tammy. He had been lost now for two years.

He had learnt how to hide from the unkind orange animals and he had managed to survive the coldest winter nights.

He had also found another house that was filled with lots of other cats. There was a kind lady there too who fed Buttons whenever he visited.

He felt lucky to have found this lady but he knew she wasn't Tammy.

The kind lady's name was Dee.

She noticed Buttons had six toes on his front left paw, so she called him Webby (like webbed feet).

Dee thought somebody would be missing this handsome cat, so she made some "Lost and Found" posters and put them up in the local streets.

Walking home from school one day, Tammy saw a poster on a tree about a tabby cat.

She jolted upright and snatched the poster off the tree. She couldn't believe her eyes. It was Buttons!

She ran home in excitement. "Mum! Mum!" she yelled, bolting into the house. "LOOK!" and she showed her mummy the poster.

Mum hugged Tammy so tight and said, "I can't believe it!"

Mummy dialled the number on the poster and spoke to the lady – Dee.

It had been two years since Buttons had vanished but now they were about to collect him.

Tammy and mummy felt excited but worried too, as Dee said that Buttons had become quite wild.

He hissed a lot and didn't let her touch him. Mummy took the pet carrier.

The surprising thing was that Dee did not live very far from Tammy so why couldn't Buttons find his way back home?

Tammy rang the bell at Dee's flat. Dee welcomed them into her home.

There were several cats in the kitchen. One of them was Buttons.

Tammy was overjoyed. She knelt down, extended her hand and gently called, "Buttons." Buttons immediately meowed, trotted over to Tammy and started rubbing against her.

"My Tammy," he thought. "I know it is you. I never forgot you." Dee was astonished at how friendly Buttons was with Tammy and how he clearly remembered her.

"I am here, Buttons," said Tammy. "I will take you home. I have missed you so much."

Tammy and mummy thanked Dee for everything she had done, then they carried Buttons back home where he belonged.

"It's a miracle, mum," said Tammy. "I know," said mum. "I really thought he had gone forever."

They arrived home and opened the door.

They let Buttons out of the pet carrier. "Welcome home, Buttons," they said.

Buttons slowly entered the house. He knew where he was.

"I am home," he thought. "Tammy is still here and she still loves me. I won't get lost again, Tammy. I hated being away from you and am so glad to be home."

"Come on, Buttons," Tammy said, "let me feed you."

Buttons remembered his bowl and his bed but, most of all, he remembered home and being loved by Tammy.

About the Creators

The Writer:
A Nursery Nurse for over a decade in an inner-city primary school, Leila Rahim has worked with children across all backgrounds. She finds engaging with children a challenging but immensely rewarding experience. All children love a good story and, taking them along the journey whilst learning, is a key feature to encourage the love of books and increasing their literacy.

The Illustrator:
A picture speaks a thousand words. This is what Mahmud Rahim has tried to achieve in producing these illustrations covering Buttons' and Tammy's journey. Whether it's a tone or particular nuance in a gait or stance, he hopes it expresses the story as intended.

First published in paperback by
Michael Terence Publishing in 2020
www.mtp.agency

Copyright © 2020 Leila Rahim

Leila Rahim has asserted the right to be identified as
the author of this work in accordance with the
Copyright, Designs and Patents Act 1988

ISBN 9781913653941

No part of this publication may be reproduced, stored in a retrieval system,
or transmitted in any form or by any means, electronic, mechanical,
photocopying, recording or otherwise, without the
prior permission of the publisher

Illustrated by Mahmud Rahim

Cover design
Copyright © 2020 Michael Terence Publishing

www.ingramcontent.com/pod-product-compliance
Lightning Source LLC
LaVergne TN
LVHW081546060526
838200LV00048B/2235